Rental Property

Complete Guide to Rental Property Investment and Management, From Beginner to Expert A-Z

Jason Cooper

Table of Contents

Introduction

Chapter 1: Why Should I Get into Rental Property Investing

Chapter 2: Picking out the Type of Property to Invest In

Chapter 3: Financing Your Rental Property

Chapter 4: The Property Search

Chapter 5: Preparing the Property to Lease Out

Chapter 6: Picking Out the Right Renal Terms.

Chapter 7: Finding Good Tenants to Protect Your Investment

Chapter 8: Your Responsibilities as a Landlord

Conclusion

its nature, the information presented is without assurance regarding its continued validity or interim quality. Trademarks that mentioned are done without written consent and can in no way be considered an endorsement from the trademark holder.

Introduction

Congratulations for purchasing your personal copy of *Rental Property: Complete Guide to Rental Property Investment and Management, From Beginner to Expert A-Z* Thank you for doing so.

The following chapters will discuss some of the many things that you need to know when it is time to start working on rental property investing. This is a fantastic thing to work on because you can get a great return on your investment, but it is important to take the right steps to help increase your profit and get some good tenants into your properties.

In this guidebook, we are going to take some time to talk about the different aspects of rental property investing. We are going to explore some of the reasons why you would want to get into this form of investing, how to pick out the right property, how to find financing, picking good tenants that will help to protect your investment, the importance of writing out a lease, and even some of your own rights as the landlord.

Rental property investing is a very secure form of investing as long as you are careful about picking a property that is a good price and you keep your other costs low with good tenants. When you are ready to get started in rental property investing, make sure to check out this guidebook and learn how to get started and see success in no time.

There are plenty of books on this subject on the market, thanks again for choosing this one! Every effort was made to ensure it is full of as much useful information as possible. Please enjoy!

Chapter 1: Why Should I Get Into Rental Property Investing

If you are looking to get into the real estate market, one of the best investment opportunities that you can choose is rental properties. You will be able to make a small amount of income from each property each month while also building up equity in the property at the same time. You will own this property the whole time, so you can do what you would like with this property, but you still get to make some money in the process and while paying off the mortgage of the property all in one.

While this is a great option for many investors because you get to earn money while owning your property, there are still quite a few things that you must deal with when it comes to working in rental properties. As the landlord, you need to keep up with your responsibilities to the tenant. You can't just hand over the keys and ignore maintenance and other issues that come up with the home. You need to make sure that the rent will be high enough that it covers your costs as well as making you an income while still being low enough to attract tenants so the home doesn't sit vacant. You also need to pick out some good tenants who will take care of the property and won't add to your workload.

Before you decide that rental property investing is the right choice for you, you need to realize that there is a lot of work that comes with this income. Too many investors think that this is any easy way to get rich without having to work, but there are various steps that you have to take, along with a lot of work, before you can even make some income. But the benefits often outweigh the work and if you are able to purchase more than one property and work with a property manager, you can get a great income going.

Benefits of rental property investing

When you get into rental properties, remember that this is going to be a type of business. You are trying to get your money to work with you so treating this as a serious matter can help you to make smart decisions when it comes to choosing properties and taking care of your asset. You will need to make sure that you provide your tenant (or the customer of your business) with a safe and nice place to live in and then they will pay you for providing this place to live in. With this perspective, there are four main benefits from going with rental properties including:

- **Tangible asset**
- **Current income**
- **Appreciation**
- **Tax advantages**

Tangible asset

One of the benefits of rental property investment is that your property is actually a tangible product, something that you are able to see and touch. There are so many investment options, like owning a part of a company, are not tangible and this can make it hard to feel like you are really doing anything with your money. Rental properties are things you can step inside of, make some changes to, and see whenever you would like. You have both the land and the home that you can work with, and you can sell it easily if something goes wrong with renting it out in order to recover some of your losses. Many new investors like to use this option because they can actually see what they are working with rather than just looking at a piece of paper.

Current income

Some of the other investment opportunities that you can pick from, such as flipping homes, won't make you money for a while. You have to make some updates to the home, ride out the market, and then wait for the home to sell. It could take a few years before you are able to see any money from your investment. But with rental properties, you can make money as soon as you find a tenant to rent out the building. The income that you make is going to vary based on the amount you charge for rent minus what you will pay for with the mortgage and the other expenses you have to pay to make sure the house stays up and running.

In the beginning, your expenses are going to be higher because you will have to pay off the mortgage with the rent, but over time this can be paid off and this means that for the same rental price, you can earn more income. Make sure that when calculating your income, though, you consider other expenses like insurance on the home, taxes, and some of the utilities that you will pay out of pocket.

If you are careful about the property that you are renting, you will make more income. The lower the taxes and the mortgage on the property, the more income you will be able to make. And if you pick tenants who stick around for a long time and don't ruin your property you will make a higher income as well.

Equity

Since you actually own the property even when a tenant is living in the property, you will be able to build up equity in the property over time. The equity is basically going to be the difference between what the property is worth and what you owe on this property. As you pay off some more of your mortgage each month, you will increase your equity. In addition, real estate is an investment that increases in value over the years, so when you combine it with paying down your mortgage, your equity can raise considerably.

But why is equity so important? There are a lot of benefits that come from using this equity. There are some landlords who will take this equity and let it build up for a little bit. Then they can get a loan in order to purchase another rental property to make some extra income each month. This is an easier form of cash flow and as long as you are good at paying back the money you borrow, it is easier than working with a bank.

If you don't end up using this equity for buying other properties, you can keep saving it up. Eventually, the home will be paid off and you can use that money as more of your income or you can sell the home for a full profit.

Tax advantages

You will find that there are many tax advantages that will come from using rental properties. Since this is actually a business so you can deduct the expenses of this business, such as maintenance of the property. You can also claim the interest rate, the taxes, and the mortgage when it is tax season. It is best to work with a tax professional so that you can learn of all the deductions that are available for your business, just make sure that you keep good records all year to make this easier.

If you do get some of these tax advantages, make sure that you use the extra money in a wise manner. You can use it to purchase another property or to build up some more equity in your property. It is not a good idea to go crazy with this, especially if you want to keep growing your investment so make a plan and put it to use.

The risks of these rental properties

There are a lot of benefits that come with using rental properties, but there are also a few things that you will need to work with and understand before you jump into this investment type. It is sometimes hard to earn an income from this option and there are many risks including:

- **Eviction expenses**
- **Attorney fees**
- **Advertising fees**
- **Liability**
- **Unexpected expenses**
- **Vacancy**

Liability

Since you are the landlord, there are going to be some circumstances that will add on expenses that you will need to deal with. For example, if there is something that happens to a tenant on your property and it was due to an oversight from you, you may have to pay some more money out of pocket. You have to keep your properties up to code all of the time because if there is something wrong, you will have to pay for it.

One thing to consider is to pick an entity for your new business. If you don't pick one, you will be considered a sole proprietorship and if one of these accidents occur, you could lose all of your income for the business as well as some of your own personal assets. An LLC is a great option because it allows you to conduct business as a sole proprietorship, but you get the benefits of being able to have protection in case something does go wrong.

Unexpected expenses

As the landlord, there are going to be times when you are dealing with situations that can cost you a lot of money. A water heater can break, some water damage comes up in the basement, you have a bad tenant that destroys a home, replacing the roof when a storm comes, or even maintenance fees can all cut into the profit that you are making. One rule of thumb to follow is that the older the home that you are dealing with, the more expenses you will need to deal with. A good way to make sure that these expenses are taken care of is to set up your own saving account and put a little bit of the rental money each month inside. Then you have some of a cushion when something does come up.

Bad tenants

One of the worst things that can happen to a landlord is bad tenants because they are going to ruin a lot of your investment, eat into your income, and just make things miserable. Often these tenants are going to cause some destruction to a bit of the property, they can be hard to get the rent from, and even some will leave the property and disappear without paying the last months' rent. There are times when you will need to call in a collection agency so that you can get this rent, but with bad tenants, it is likely that you will not see this money. Bad tenants often mean that you are going to have a lot of wasted time and money on your investment.

Vacancy

While it is best if you are able to keep the property full with tenants as much as possible, there are times when the property becomes empty in between tenants. It is a good idea to build up a little bit of your savings so that you can pay the mortgage while searching for a tenant. If you have taken good care of the property and keep the rent at a reasonable price, you will be able to find someone new to move in. But there are times when you may have to pay for a few months of the mortgage on your own in between the tenants.

There are many things that you are going to enjoy when it comes to working with rental property investment. It is a great way to make an income, especially if you have more than one property, while still owning the property and earning some equity through each mortgage payment. There are some downsides that you have to consider and you must be well prepared before you are able to do well in this market. But if you take care of your assets, pick some good tenants, and make sure that you put aside some money each month for those expenses, and you will be well on your way to seeing success.

Chapter 2: Picking Out the Type of Property to Invest In

There are so many great types of properties that you can use in order to invest in real estate and start working with rental properties, and it really just depends on how much income you would like to make and how much work you want to put into it. Some of the options that you can choose from include commercial properties, condos, apartment buildings, duplexes and triplexes, and single family homes. Let's take a look at how all of these work so you can make the decision on which one is best for you.

Single family homes

Many beginners like to start with just single family homes because they are easy to keep up with and you only have one tenant, though if the place becomes vacant, no one is there to help cover the rent so it is your responsibility. The tenant will often stick around for some time so you won't always need to worry about finding a new tenant. Some of the benefits of going with a single family home include:

- You will have less work because you are taking care of just one property rather than a bunch of them together.

- The renter will usually take care of setting up and paying the utilities, which means that you get to keep more of the rent.

- You will be able to pick what size of home you would like to work with. you can pick whether there is a finished basement, how many bedrooms and bathrooms, and more.

- You only have to watch out for one renter, and in single family homes, they are usually pretty reliable on paying their rent, which means you hardly ever have to chase after any of them.

Duplex and Triplex

The next type of property that you can choose is a multi-family dwelling. This one is kind of like the middle ground of single family and apartment buildings. You will have everyone in the same building and these often attract some of the steadier tenants that you want, but you can earn more money because more people live inside the same building. These would be pretty comfortable and provide enough room for a family, but you could have two to four families paying rent on a building that is not much more than a single family home. Even if one of the parts is vacant for a bit, you will still have others who can help to take care of the mortgage. Some of the benefits of these properties include:

- You can live in one of the parts of this building while someone else (or multiple tenants depending on the size) rent out the other part and pay your mortgage.

- You are able to rent to more than one tenant at the same time, which helps you to earn more income.

- You still only need to take care of the one building to be successful.

Apartment Buildings

Apartment buildings can be another option that you use in this investing and they can cost a lot of money. Most beginners will not start with this because they cost a lot and they take quite a bit of work. Maintaining them can be harder and keeping turnover rates low can sometimes be a challenge mainly because of the type of people who live in these properties. But if you are able to come up with the money to start one and you are good at keeping the units filled and well maintained, you can make a huge profit on just one building. Some of the benefits that you can get from this type of property includes:

It is common for investors with apartment buildings to work with management groups. This allows for more investors to work together and lowers the risk compared to other options.

You are able to make quite a bit more money than the other options because there are so many units that are available. If you have 100 units in a building, you are making quite a bit more than on a single family or a triplex. This makes it easier to pay down the mortgage and to keep costs low.

All of your units are going to be in the same place, so maintaining the outside will not be that difficult.

Condos

Next on the list are condos. There are many individuals who like the idea of renting out condos to make some money on this investment. Many of the elderly like to move into these condos because they are comfortable and the landlord, or you, will take care of the maintenance and the upkeep for the residents inside. Those who move into the condos often have a decent income and will pay more for the comfort of these properties as well as the convenience of having someone else do the work for them. As long as you keep them nice, you can make a great income from them. Some of the benefits that you get for renting out condos include:

- The condo is technically still a single unit, so there isn't too much extra care that you need to do with them. You can choose to rent them out as vacation rentals or to full-time residents.

- The maintenance with a condo will be taken care of with homeowners' associations in the area, so this can save you some money and time.

- It is possible to get a condo that is attached to your own living area, so you can check in on your tenants whenever or you can make sure that the rent covers your living expenses to be there.

Commercial property

If you would like to take a slightly different route to rental property investing while still making a good amount of money, commercial properties may be the answer that you are looking for. These properties allow you to work with different businesses who want to make sure that they have a physical location for their stores and they likely will want to stay in one place for a long time. This provides a lot of stability for you, but if a business does shut down or leave, it is sometimes hard to fill this space up again. It will cost you a bit more to purchase these properties so funding can be hard, but with the stability and the good rent you can get from businesses, it is often a good investment. Some of the benefits that you can get from using commercial properties include:

- You may be able to split up a commercial property so that more than one business rents out of the same place. This makes it easier to pay down your mortgage and gives you more rental income.

- Most businesses are willing to pay a decent rent to you. This is a good source to work with if you want to make this your full-time income.

As you can see, there are many different options that you can choose from when it comes to picking out the rental property that you want to work with. Some are going to provide a higher income potential than others, but there are more risks and more work involved with them so often it is based on your personal preference. Take the time to pick out which type of property you want to work with and then go out with a realtor and find the property that is best for your needs.

Chapter 3: Financing Your Rental Property

Once you have an idea of the strategy that you would like to work with, it is time to talk about financing. If you are able to save up the amount of money that you need, this is the best option. You won't have to worry about paying the bank at all and there is no need to worry about interest adding up.

You can start making more income right from the beginning, minus the unexpected expenses and some taxes and insurance. Of course, most people who are ready to start investing in real estate don't have this much money saved up (it is pretty expensive to purchase a house or an apartment building for example) so they will need to find some form of financing to help them to make the purchase.

As you get into this journey, it is a good idea to look at various funding sources to find out which one will offer you the best terms and the best rates to help save you money. Also, make sure that your credit score is in good order, that you feel out the applications thoroughly, and even have a marketing plan in place to show potential investors that you are serious about your new business.

Some of the best sources of financing that you can use to help fund your rental properties include:

Banks and credit unions

One of the first places that you will stop in order to finance your rental property is a bank or credit union. These have a long application process, but they have the best terms when it comes to interest rates, security, and length of the loan so that you can save some money. You will most likely need to go in and fill out a lengthy application, provide proof of income, have a good credit score, and even show your marketing plan to prove that you are serious about this investment.

Banks can be tough to get funding from because so many people come to them for help and they want to make sure that they are going to get their money back. If you want to increase your chances of getting the funding that is needed, make sure that you fill out the application completely and that you provide all the information that is asked for. Picking out a bank or credit union that you use is also a good idea because they are familiar with you and will be more willing to work with you.

Independent investors in your area

In some cases, there are independent investors who are looking to grow their portfolio, but they are not able to do some of the work of real estate on their own. They may be willing to provide you with some of the funding that you need in order to earn a good return on their investment while letting you take care of all the hard work. They basically take the risk while you are doing the work.

These investors can be a great resource for you, and it is very important to act professionally when talking to them. Have a presentation set up that shows what your goals are and the terms that you would like to use when paying back the amount that they loan. Be ready for some negotiations so that both parties are able to reach an agreement that is satisfactory.

Family and friends

If you have some friends and family who are willing to help you out or who would like to start investing themselves without having to do the work, this can be a good place to get some funding for your ventures. Often these are going to offer some good terms because these are people you know.

When working with people you know about funding for your rental properties, make sure that you set up some terms and conditions, such as how much interest you will pay them and when the full amount is due back, right from the beginning. Even though they are people you know, it is important to put these figures in writing so everyone is on the same page in terms of expectations and there aren't any hard feelings between the two groups.

Finding funding for the rental property, especially if you haven't built up any equity yet, can be an important step to taking care of your investment. There are many options to try and picking one that gives you the best terms is perfect for getting you on the right foot to success in this business and can even determine how much income you will get out of the whole process.

Chapter 4: The Property Search

Once you have the financing in order and you know how much you will be able to get from the bank and how much you are able to afford, it is time to look for a property. There are several methods that you can use in order to find the right property that will be a good price, in a nice neighborhood, and will attract the tenants that you would like. Many beginners' like to work with a real estate agent because they know the area and can often find some of the best information about deals in the area and can help you determine if a property is right for your needs.

Places to look for homes

There are a variety of places you can search in order to find a property for your rental income. You do need to be careful with the homes you pick, though; just because they are nice doesn't mean they are priced competitively enough that you can make an income from the rent. But with some good researching skills and some patience, you will be able to find the perfect property. Some of the resources that you can use to find a good property include:

- Your realtor: many times those who are looking for a new property, whether to purchase for themselves or for an investment, will go with a realtor. The realtor knows a lot of information about your area and can find some of the properties that you may have missed.

- The MLS: one of the first places you should go to find a home. All homes that are listed with any of the agents in your area will be listed on this database. This can also be helpful if you are looking in a different town for the homes because you can just see which ones are listed nationally. Your realtor will often pick this option as well to help you find some of the properties that you want.

- Online home listing sites: in addition to the MLS, there are a few other places you can look to find homes that are available. Look on sites like auction.com, Zillow.com, and more to see if there are some good deals on the homes you would like to purchase.

- Driving around town: some of the best deals in purchasing real estate is to look for homes that are sold by the owner rather than by the realtor. Usually, the sellers have to pay their realtor a percentage of the sale, so this increases how much they will try to ask for the home. But for sale by owner homes have fewer expenses so that savings can be given to you.

- Networking: sometimes it is the people you know who can help you to find the right property. If you know a lot of people in the real estate industry and around town, you may hear some of the rumors about a home that may be coming for sale and at a good price.
You may be able to talk to them about purchasing the home before it even gets to the market. Some of the best sales in real estate never even get listed online or with an agent and if you are good at networking, you will be able to find them.

- Craigslist: Craigslist can sometimes be a great place to start with finding the right rental property for you. Some for sale by owners are listed there because it is free to do the listing and can reach a large audience. Be careful when using this option, though. Never send money to someone through craigslist and always go and take a look at the property ahead of time.

Finding the right property can take some time. You want to find a home that someone else would be willing to rent from you and you need to make sure that it is at a good price so you can still make an income. But if you look around at all these different options and keep your eyes open, you will find something that you really like.

Meeting your criteria

Before you get into a home, you should create a list of criteria that you would like the home to meet. How much will you be willing to pay for the property, how many bedrooms and bathrooms do you want, do you want it to have a basement, is there a backyard? You need to write all of this down before you even step foot into the first home on your search.

It is common to get into a home and fall in love with it, but it may be too expensive for your price range and you won't be able to rent it out and still make a profit. Or there may be so much work to it, it may be missing some things, or there are other issues that don't meet up with your criteria and could cost you a lot of wasted time and money.

Some of the requirements that you may want to stick with if you would like to purchase a home for a single family include a home that has three bedrooms, is near a school, and has both a yard and a garage. If you want to just have a smaller family or single people in the home, the criteria would change a little bit. Know what kind of customer you would like to work with because this will often determine what kind of property you decide to go with.

There are some times when you can vary off your requirements a bit, such as being slightly out of the neighborhood that you want to save some money, but for the most time, you should bring this list of criteria to all the house searches that you do. This helps you to keep on track and will help you to avoid getting a property that won't work for your rental needs.

Picking out the property that you will purchase can be an exciting time, but there are many things that you have to consider to make sure that you get the property that is nice, that will attract the right tenants, and will still be at a good cost so that you can pick a competitive rent and still make an income. You need to take your time, run the numbers on each property, and make some important decisions to help protect your investment and get the right rental income to work for you.

Chapter 5: Preparing the Property to Lease Out

Once you have been able to pick out a new property to use as your rental investment, it is time to make sure that the property is ready to rent out. You want to make sure that the property looks nice to a potential renter so that you can get them into the building, keep them comfortable so they stay in the property for longer, and ensure that you make some income off the work.

A good place to get started is to look at the property and pretend that you would be moving in here. What are some basic things that you can do to the property that would help to make it more comfortable?
What are some of the things that you see that may turn people off of the property? You can make some of these changes in order to get the property to look nice and pleasing to a potential renter.

To make the potential renter more comfortable in the property, make sure to take care of the following things:

Fix anything that is broken

In most cases, if the property was a good deal, it is because there are at least a few things that you must fix and clean up around the home. You may need to spend some time painting some of the rooms, fixing some of the spots that are inside the wall or changing out the appliances that don't work. These are things that you should have added into your consideration when choosing whether to get this property or not because it is going to cost you a little more and this should be determined by the price.

If there are a lot of things inside of the property that are worn down and broken, it is going to be hard to get others to want to live inside of it. Make sure that it all looks nice and neat and fix anything that is broken and doesn't work as nicely as it should.

Make sure the home meets all codes

Every home needs to meet certain codes before you are able to rent that property to others. If you don't fix some of the code violations, or you don't get the new violations fixed as quickly as you can, it is possible for the tenant to sue you and that could be the end of your investment.
You should be able to avoid most of these problems by doing an inspection before you made the purchase so that will save you a little bit of a headache. With that being said, if you own the property for some time, some new violations that come up later on and you need to get them fixed as quickly as possible.

Even once you get a tenant into the property, it is a good idea to schedule in some regular checks on the different features of the home. this could include some things like the heater, the water, and the electricity. This helps you to check out each of these items to make sure they are up to the proper codes.

Make sure that you tell the tenant when you plan to do this, you can't just walk into the property because the tenant does have some rights. But if you give them a written notice ahead of time or add it into the lease, then the tenant will know when you are coming and you can make sure the home is safe.

Change the locks

Any and all locks that are in the home and the garage need to be changed. This includes the ones for all the doors in the property, the mailboxes, the sheds, the gates, and even the garage if there are keys to this. This should be done after you make the purchase and after each tenant leaves. This helps you to know that only the tenant and you have the right keys to this property so that no one else is able to get into the property.

Clean the carpets

It is very much worth your time to call in a professional to help you to take care of those carpets. There is so much that can get into the carpets over time from bad smells, stains, and more that a professional carpet cleaner who does a full steam, as well as a shampoo of the carpets, will be able to massively enhance the overall look of the house.
In some cases, you may choose to do some of this carpet cleaning on your own, but it is really going to make a difference if you hire a professional to help you get this done.

You may want to consider doing this each time that a tenant moves out of your property. This will make sure that all of the messes that they do to the property are taken care of and that the home looks really nice again when a new potential tenant comes in to look at it.

It doesn't take too much time to get the carpets done, but it can make a huge difference in how you find a new tenant.

Do some of the yard work

While the inside of the property is very important, don't underestimate the importance of taking care of the outside of the home as well. Your potential tenants want to feel comfortable on the property and if you leave it looking run down and a big mess on the outside, it is not going to matter how nice the inside looks. Luckily, making some changes to the landscaping and doing some yard work doesn't have to cost you a lot of money.

First, start with mowing the lawn, trimming any bushes and trees that may be a bit overgrown, pull out the weeds, and fix anything that you see is broken, if you notice there are a lot of plants that look dead or dying, pull them out.

You can even add in some other greenery and some flowers to make the home look more inviting. Don't forget to spray of the sidewalks to get the dirt to leave, keep leaves out of the yard, and just do some little fixes to make the home look nicer.

Change out the filters

If the home has been empty for some time, it is a good idea to change out the filters. You would be surprised at how dirty these things can get in no time and they really do affect how the ventilation system will work in your home. Before a new tenant moves in and on regular intervals afterward, make sure to clean out the vents and the area around them to keep the system working well.

Disposable filters are the best because you won't have to clean these out and most landlords find these are the easy ones to maintain.

Clean the interior

A good cleaning in the home can make a big difference on how nice it looks. It is best to go with a professional service to do this so that they can get the grime and the dirt that is hidden in the home, but the potential tenant may be able to notice. The walls should be wiped down well, the windows cleaned, and some care should be given to cleaning the appliances. Mop the floors or carpet clean your carpets. This does take a lot of time, but your tenant is definitely going to notice.

Add some more lights

Some tenants are not too thrilled with a home that doesn't have a lot of lights in it because it does make it hard to see inside the property and can make your property look smaller. If you notice that some of the lightbulbs have gone out in the home, make sure to get them replaced.

Add some extra lamps in some rooms that may not have as many lights or windows and keep the curtains opened up so that the natural light can come through. In some cases, you can find brighter bulbs that will help to make the room look better and if you need to paint a few of the rooms, go with lighter colors to help with this.

Don't forget those ceiling fans

Never forget to spend some time cleaning the tops of the ceiling fans. These are often dusty and bad in no time and if a potential tenant sees this, it can look bad. First, get a wipe and learn how you should clean the tops and the sides of the fans. Then double check to make sure they are working or if it is time to replace some of the blades for your tenants.

Check the screens

Now it is time to check on your doors and windows. If these don't have some screens in place already, it is worth your time to invest in a few. You just need to measure out the space that you have available and then go to a local store to find the best screen replacements for your needs. Many homeowners want to be able to open up these windows without dust and bugs getting inside.

If the home already has some doors and windows inside, you need to inspect all of these. If there are holes, tears, and rips that you are not able to repair pretty quickly, it is a good idea to get them replaced. Also, you should check around the edges to see that all of these screens fit into their respective places properly. Wipe down all of the edges so that they look clean and nice.

Spray for the pests

Depending on how old the home is, how long it was sitting empty before you made a purchase, and even the area you live in, it is important to spray for pests. Sometimes there are pests inside and they try to make this their new home.

Even if someone is already living in the home or lived in it when you made the purchase, it is a good precaution to go through and spray for these pests to keep the home safe.

These are mostly little fixes that you will be able to do to make the home look nicer and to ensure that you are able to rent it out at a good price. They may be little things, but they are going to make a big difference to a potential tenant who wants the home to look nice and neat.

Chapter 6: Picking Out the Right Rental Terms

After you have had some time to fix up the property and it is ready to have a tenant inside, you need to figure out a few numbers. You probably took some time to think about these numbers ahead of time when thinking about how much you wanted to make the purchase for, but now it is time to really get the numbers down. As a landlord, you want to make sure that you bring in as much profit as possible, but if you place the rent too high or above market value for its type, you will find that tenants will not want to live there.

So the first thing that you need to consider is how much you will spend on all the expenses to maintain the home. this includes the mortgage payment that you do each month, the insurance for the home, the taxes, some money that you put back in case things break or need to be fixed in the home, and any other fees or expenses that you are planning to pay.

Remember that you need to keep this number lower than what you will charge for rent, with some margin for the profit you want to earn as well.

Once the amount of expenses you would need to take care of is figured out, you need to determine how much you would prefer to be able to earn in income each month. This number does need to be reasonable.

On one single family property, it is not possible to make a thousand dollars every month just in income. A couple hundred per property is usually about right for starting out unless you were able to get a really good deal on the property to start with.

The market value of your particular property is also going to make a difference on how much you are going to charge for the rent. If you find that with the market value, the rent for other homes in your area that are similar to your property go for $900 a month, this is a good starting point.

Most of the time tenants will not pay higher because they are able to find other places that are going to be less expensive but still nice. If you calculated out the expenses right and $900 ends up being way above what your expenses are, that just means more money in your pocket or a more attractive rental price for the tenant.

If you were able to purchase the home below its market value, you should be just fine with getting the expenses to be lower than or line up to the amount that you will be able to charge for rent. If you purchase a home that is way too close or above the market value, it can make it challenging to price the rent so it is high enough to earn the profit that you want but still low enough that you will attract in some of the potential tenants that you want.

The lower the purchase price the easier you will find it is to make some profit off these properties.

These are calculations that you need to do before you actually purchase the house so that you can actually make a smart decision on the purchase and not find out later on that you got it for too much and can't make a profit. Before making the purchase, sit down and find out how much the mortgage, taxes, and insurance are (at a minimum) on this property at its current price. Then you can also look at some other properties in the area, or ask around, that are similar to yours and find out how much they are charging for rent each month.

This can make it easier to determine if you are actually going to make some profit in this game or if you will be stuck with a home and no income from it.

Any time that you are unsure about what the market price is for other similar rentals, a good place to check is your local government office or online. You will be able to look at charts about the average rental income in this area and you can look it all over to find out what a good rental price will be.

It is a good idea to stick near these prices in order to maximize your profit will still enticing tenants to pick your property.

Sometimes you will need to compete with some of the other rental properties out there. This can be hard when you first get started because you may be competing with some who can lower their prices because they purchased the home and have the mortgage paid off, but you need to look at the averages of the rent in your area for similar homes and try to do your best to compete.

If you planned everything out the right way, you will find that it is pretty easy to get the rental price that is the average in your area to match up with your expenses and a little income left over. But if you just make a purchase without doing the research ahead of time, you may be disappointed and not be able to get anything out of this investment.

Picking out the price of your property is going to make a big difference on whether or not you make an income and whether someone will choose to rent out the home for you. Make sure that you run all of your numbers before making a purchase so that you have a good idea of what is going on in the market and you can actually make your income without having to way overcharge a potential tenant.

Chapter 7: Finding Good Tenants to Protect Your Investment

At this point, we have taken a look at what types of properties you can purchase, how to find the right financing for your goals, how to pick out a property and find the one that is right for you, how to fix it up to really entice your potential tenant and even how to price the rent the right way so that tenants will pick your property over another one that is similar.

But now it is time to start looking at how you will be able to find the good tenants to live in your building.

It is never a good idea to decide to just go with the first tenants that walk in the door. Bad tenants are going to miss out on rent, leave the home without paying their rent at all, and they often destroy some of the property that you are dealing with so you have to work with a big mess that costs money and takes up time rather than getting more tenants in there right away.

On the other hand, good tenants are going to take care of your properties, often stay for a couple of years for a good steady income, and will pay their rent on time.

How to find the good tenants

If you are able to find good tenants to live in your property, it is going to make a big difference when you first get going on your rental properties. The good tenants are the ones who will always pay their rent on time each month, who are willing to take care of the property and not cause more than normal wear and tear damage on the property, and will only bother you if there is really something wrong with your property that you are supposed to fix.

They won't be a big bother, you barely need to check on them, and you will find that they stick around on the property for a long time.

The problem with this is that it is really tough to find these good tenants to live in your property. All people who have spent some time working in real estate investing have horror stories about tenants who were horrible and really destroyed their investment. So you always need to be on the lookout to try and keep these bad tenants out of your properties.

You may find that it is impossible to avoid the bad tenants all of the time, but if you take the right precautions along the way, it is less likely that you will let them in

So when you are ready to find some good tenants to live in the property, the first step that you need to take is listing the home. You should take your time to really showcase the home, writing out a good description, adding in some great pictures, and showing as much detail as possible.

The good tenants are going to be drawn in with properties that are well maintained, found in some of the better neighborhoods in town, and that look nice which is why the pictures can be so important to add. You should also try to post this on a few different sites so that it is more likely that the perfect tenant is going to be able to see it.

While you are writing out the property listing, take some time to write out the requirements that you have for living on the property. There are several benefits to this including saving time on some of the questions that will be asked as well as helping to keep some of the bad tenants out.

For example, in this part you can include things like security deposits, how long you want the lease to last, the rental price, and whether you allow animals on the property. This is going to help you to avoid some confusion later on with your tenants.

Give it a few days for some potential tenants to get ahold of you and then the applications will start to come in. You need to look at each one individually. Some tenants are going to look great on paper (although you may be surprised at how many you can eliminate from their applications), but these applications often don't go too much in depth about the tenant so sometimes it is easy for those bad ones to hide their true selves and look good on the application. Always take the time to double check the information that you are provided before starting.

One thing that you should never miss out on is doing a background check on any applicant that you are looking to rent out the property to. There is so much information that can come up on these background checks and they can really help you to figure out if the tenant is going to be a good one for you.

One thing that you will find in the background check is a bit of information on that applicants' credit history, including if they pay their rent on time to other landlords and if they have had a steady work history.

If it is possible, call up any of the landlords that the tenant lived with in the past. These landlords will be pretty honest with you and will tell you whether the applicant will not pay their rent well or if there are other factors that you need to be worried about.

This does take a little bit of extra work to get done, but it is going to help you weed out some of those bad tenants right from the beginning. In some cases, when a tenant finds out that you automatically do background checks on all potential tenants, they may decide to not even submit an application because they know what you will find.

This can save you a bit of time on some bad applicants, but be aware that some will still try to get through so make sure to do a background check on all of the potential tenants just to be on the safe side. You can do the background checks on your own if you would like, but most landlords will choose to hire a company who will be able to get the work done quickly and for a good cost.

In addition, you should consider making the tenants give you three or four references that are not related to the tenant. This again may turn away some of the applicants, but these are people you didn't really want to have on the property anyway. The best references are going to be a professional acquaintance, a co-worker, or a landlord of the tenant.

A bad reference is going to have trouble finding just three references that would speak well of them and they will either try to not provide these to you or when you give them a call, they don't have as much nice stuff to say as you would hope. Make sure to actually call up these references to make sure that they have nice things to say about the potential tenant and to see if they are actually real.

As a beginner, you may be excited to get that property filled up and you want to just start getting the tenants in there right away. But this is setting you up for disaster if you don't take the right steps to ensure, as much as possible, that a good tenant gets into the building. With a little bit of research and a bit of patience, you will see that it isn't too bad to find a good tenant you can rely on.

Creating the lease

Before the tenant moves into the property, you need to create a lease. This is going to help protect the tenant as well as the landlord in this agreement because each party knows what is expected of them from the very beginning. You should never allow a new tenant into the property without having them sign the lease and making sure that they understand what is inside of it.

You can choose to create your very own lease, but often hiring an attorney to create the document so that it is legal can help. A few of the things that you should include in the lease would be:

The terms of this agreement: you can have a standard terms of agreement that you use or if there was something in particular that you talked about with this tenant, make sure it is in the lease. When you write it down, the words become legal and everyone is on the right page from the beginning.

Identify each party: you need to clearly state who the tenant and the landlord are and then add the physical address of your property in there as well.

How long the lease lasts: most residential leases last a year, but sometimes you can change this around to be just six months or even up to two years. You should write down the date that the lease begins on and when it should end so no one has to try and remember the exact date on their own. You can even include some information on renewing the lease when this time period ends.

Rental price: the tenant should be able to find out how much the rent is for the property each month. You can also let them know if there are particular rules on paying the lease (like if you only accept cash or check).

Security deposit: you should write out how much the security deposit is going to be. You may choose to leave this part blank so that you can offer some promotions that will bring in some of the tenants, like lowering the security deposit.

List what the parties pay for: if you will pay off the utilities out of the rent, you need to write this out. But if you require that the tenant deals with their own utilities, you need to write this in the lease as well.

Talk about subleasing: most landlords will not allow their tenant to sublease the property. Subleasing is when the tenant gets someone else to lease this property, usually to make their own profit. Include this clause in the lease that subleasing is not allowed. You can allow for the tenant to find a new tenant if they need to leave before the lease is over, but state that each of the tenants need to put in an application and pass a background check with you.

Dispute resolution: provide some information to the tenant on how both parties will resolve disputes as they come up. You will be able to provide them with the information they need on who they should contact, what forms they can fill out, or any other information to help with this.

Lease termination: there can be times when either the tenant or the landlord wants to terminate the lease. List out the exceptions for the lease right at the beginning. Also, you can list some of the financial consequences if your tenant doesn't break the lease properly.

If you are trying to keep your costs down, it is possible to pick out a template to write out this lease, but there are times when there will be questions of the legality of it. Talking to your attorney and getting a standard lease may cost a bit more, but it a much better option.

Your attorney will be able to draft up a legal lease that you are able to use with each tenant, which can be really helpful when you go through more tenants, such as a multi-family dwelling.

The lease may not seem like it is really that necessary or important, but it really protects both you and the tenant while they reside in the property. You are going to enjoy a bit of security while the tenant is on the property, or at least get some compensation if they leave before the lease and you will have some options if the property is destroyed by the tenant.

In addition, the tenant knows that you won't just randomly kick them out of the property and they know that you will take proper care of the property while they live there.

Creating and signing a lease may seem like it is a lot of work to get through it all, but it is important for providing the right protection to you and the tenant. If you find that there is a tenant who doesn't want to sign a lease, you should be wary because it is there for their protection as well and it could mean a lot of wasted time and energy on your side. Talk to an attorney to get the lease set up and make sure that your tenant has read through and understands the lease before letting them move in.

Chapter 8: Your Responsibilities as a Landlord

As the landlord, there are a few different responsibilities that you will need to take on as well. You can't just let the tenant into the building and then walk away and have nothing to do with the property other than collecting the rent each month. There are a few responsibilities that will be outlined in your lease and that you are responsible for handling.

The tenant will, for example, expect you to do a bit in order to maintain the property and you must know some of the tenant and landlord laws that are in your city or your area.

Responsibilities of the landlord

Since you own the property, you expect that the tenant is going to pay their rent and that they will not cause unneeded damage to the property. But the tenant has some expectations from you as well. The rules are going to change depending on where you live and your laws, but some of the most common responsibilities of the landlord include:

Manage the security deposit

The landlord is able to charge a security deposit if they would like, but they do not own it. Rather, it is kind of like a security blanket for the landlord in case some bad damage is done on the property or the tenant runs off before the lease is done. The tenant will pay this before moving in and the landlord will place it into a trust where they are not able to touch it.

If your tenant does well with paying their rent and they keep the property looking nice, the landlord will return this deposit once the tenant moves out. But if there are some problems with the tenant not paying their rent or they cause a lot of damage that is not normal wear and tear on the property, the landlord is able to take this money out of the trust and use it to recover some of these costs.

You must make sure that you follow any local laws in terms of how much security deposit you are able to store, how you can store this deposit, and how to return the deposit.

Obligations to disclose the owner

All of the tenants that you place into the property are allowed to know who actually owns the property. The landlord needs to release the names as well as the addresses of those who manage this property, who is going to make repairs, who can collect rent, and what party is going to handle the complaints that can come up. This is information that the landlord will write out and then provide to the tenant before they move in. If some changes happen with any of this information, the landlord will need to notify the tenant.

Obligation of possession of the unit

This one sounds complicated, but it really just means that as the landlord, you are responsible for having the unit vacant and ready for the new tenant on the move in day that both of you agreed on. You are able to show off the property and take applications for a new tenant while the previous tenant still lives inside, but when it is time for your new tenant to move in, the property needs to be vacant.

If this unit is not fully ready, the tenant has the right to pursue some legal action.

In addition, the landlord has some legal actions that they can use as well. If someone who doesn't live in this unit, or a squatter, is found inside of this unit, the landlord has the right to pursue legal action. If the landlord ends up winning this, they could be given some damages for their time and effort.

Maintain the property

It is the responsibility of the landlord to maintain the property. The tenant can't go through and purposely destroy this property and when they leave, there should only be some normal wear and tear on the property.

But if something breaks in the property, such as the heater, you as the landlord will need to take care of it. You are responsible for keeping the property clean, safe, and habitable for the tenants and you need to check all the codes on the property are up to date. You can also perform any repairs that are needed, provide running water, provide trash receptacles, and do some of the other work that was discussed for the lease.

Limitation of liability

If there is something that you and the tenant agreed upon and placed in the lease, you need to follow through on them. If there are issues that are in the landlord and tenant law, you will need to do these as well. The liability of the landlord to do this will end if the landlord sells the property, just as long as they let the tenant know that someone else is managing or owning the property. So if the landlord promised to check up on the heater each year and they sell the property, as long as they tell the tenant, they will be fine.

When a new landlord takes over the property, they will need to stick with the terms that are in the lease. If there are some changes that the new landlord would like to work with, they need to provide the changes in writing to the tenant and then give the tenant a bit of time to either make changes to follow these new terms or to move out.

Of course, each local area and state will have variations on these kinds of laws so before you start renting out a property, you need to make sure that you are up to date on these laws so that you save money and provide your tenants with a safe and comfortable place to live.

Growing your portfolio

After you have owned this first property for some time, you will have a pretty steady income and if you planned out things in the proper way, you have some equity in the home and maybe even some savings that you can use to help grow your portfolio.

Once you are pretty comfortable with the tenant that you have in the first property as well as the workload that you are dealing with and you want to take on some more and increase your income, it is time to grow the portfolio a little bit and then add in some more rental properties to help your investment to grow.

With the second property that you want to use, you will need to follow some of the same steps. You will want to find a property that is a good deal, fits your budget, and will not require too much work for you to make nice. Remember that you are already working with one rental property and you need to take this into consideration when picking out a second or a third property to add to the portfolio. Also, consider whether you will be able to handle the costs of both properties until you find tenants for the second one as well. It is a great idea to add more properties to this kind of investment, but you need to think it through carefully and not get too carried away or you could lose both properties.

As you get more comfortable with your rental properties and take on more of them, you may want to consider hiring a property manager to help out. They will take care of some of the work for you, such as collecting the rent for you, making repairs, and helping you to find new tenants.

If you have five or more properties, this can become a lot of work, especially if you are still working for your regular full-time income. You can hire a professional who is able to take this all on so that you can concentrate on purchasing other properties and growing the portfolio even more.

Make sure that you find a good property manager, one who charges competitive rates and who isn't running their own rental properties at the same time. With their help, you can continue to make your income and taking care of your tenants while you continue to grow your portfolio.

Working in rental properties can be a great way to make some money, especially when you learn how to add on more than one property, and it can be a great challenge. If you think through all of the work that you will need to do for this process, find a property that is in good working order and is a great deal, and you are able to find some good tenants, and you are ready to make a good income in your real estate investment in no time!

Conclusion

Thank for making it through to the end of **Rental Property: Complete Guide to Rental Property Investment and Management, From Beginner to Expert A-Z.**

Hope it was informative and able to provide you with all of the tools you need to achieve your goals.

The next step is to get out there and start investing in your own rental property. It may take you some time to find a property that is going to work for your needs and will help you to make a good rental income, but once you find some and fix it up to impress the tenants, you will find that this income source is easy to work with.

This guidebook has provided you with some of the best tips that you can follow when it is time to start working on rental properties. From picking out the property that you would like to work with to getting the financing, fixing up the home, and even finding some good tenants and your own responsibilities as the landlord. You have gone from a beginner to expert in no time and now should be almost ready to take on your own rental properties. Congratulations!

Finally, if you found this book useful in any way, a review on Amazon is always appreciated!

Made in the USA
San Bernardino, CA
27 April 2017